The Cherry Blossom Festival

Written by Janine Scott
Photography by Paul Dymond

Japan

Haruna loves it when spring
comes. She lives in the north
of Japan, which can be very cold.
Spring brings warmer weather
and beautiful cherry blossoms.
For one special day of friendship
and fun, Haruna and her family
take time out from their busy
lives in the city of Sapporo
to enjoy the ancient traditions
of Japan.

friendship making and keeping friends

Contents

The Cherry Blossom Festival

Haruna and her sister, Shiori, live in the Land of Flowers, as Japan is sometimes called. They live in a high-rise apartment in Sapporo, which is on the island of Hokkaido. Their favorite time of year is during the cherry blossom festival. It is a great time for flowers, food, family, friends, and fun!

Does your country have a national flower? What symbols are important in your country?

The cherry blossom is a well-known symbol of Japan. It is the most admired of all flowers. It is featured in songs and poems and on clothing and pottery. It has long been a custom in Japan to welcome spring by enjoying the cherry blossoms. People call this celebration of cherry blossoms *hanami*. In Sapporo, many families gather for hanami. Haruna and her family prepare a picnic to eat at the park while they admire the beautiful blossoms

custom   a traditional way of doing things

People all over Japan become very excited about the cherry blossoms. Radio and television stations give reports about where and when the cherry trees will be blooming. Some cherry trees flower for several weeks. Other cherry trees bloom for only a few days. Some people travel from place to place, following the flowering season.

Haruna and her family arrive at the park early. It is very busy by mid-morning. As they eat and drink, they admire the trees, which are mostly *yaezakura*. This means the blossoms have more than five petals. Some kinds of blossoms have ten, twenty, and even one hundred petals.

In the same park, trees can bloom at different times. Trees in sunny spots grow blossoms sooner than trees in the shade.

Southern Japan has warmer weather than northern Japan, and the cherry trees can start blooming as early as January. The trees in the northern part of Japan often start flowering as late as May.

A Snow Festival

In addition to the cherry blossom festival in the spring, Sapporo holds its famous snow festival during winter. This tradition began in the 1950s when a group of high school students built six snow sculptures in Sapporo's Odori Park. The students and their sculptures created so much interest that the event has continued year after year. The sculptures get bigger and better each year, too. Today, the festival is held for an entire week at three different sites in Sapporo.

Today is a very special day for Haruna and Shiori, not only because the cherry blossoms are blooming, but also because it is the fifth day of May. In Japan, this is Children's Day and a national holiday.

On Children's Day, people fly special windsocks outside their houses and over rivers and lakes. The windsocks are in the shape of carp, a fish related to the goldfish. The carp stands for strength and courage. People hope that their children will swim through life and overcome difficulties, just as the carp swims against the strong, fast-flowing currents.

This difficult traditional Japanese game is very popular at festival time. Children try to catch goldfish with a net made from very thin paper. If they are able to catch a fish, they are allowed to keep it.

In poems and songs, the life of a samurai warrior was often compared with the short life of the cherry blossom. Here Haruna wears a samurai paper helmet. These helmets, worn on Children's Day, were originally supposed to make boys grow strong like warriors.

In the past, people celebrated their sons on the 5th of May. Daughters were honored on the 3rd of March, during the Doll Festival. However, this all changed in 1948. Both boys and girls are now honored on the 5th of May.

samurai a traditional Japanese soldier or warrior

Haruna and Shiori had their photos taken in this photo booth and then decorated the pictures with special pens. The photos printed out as stickers.

Not everything on this day is traditionally Japanese! Haruna's parents bought cotton candy for a treat, and Haruna and Shiori played computer games.

These drums are part of a video game. The idea is to beat the drum in time to your favorite song to score points. Two people can compete against each other.

The cherry blossom festival gives people all over Japan a chance to celebrate Japanese traditions. For many people, the old ways are no longer a major part of their everyday lives. Today, many children now play with robotic toys and computer games and watch cartoons on television. The performances in the park at the blossom festival provide a glimpse of life in traditional Japan. Many festivals around the country put on displays of Japanese music and dance, flower arranging, martial arts, and many other activities that are special to Japan.

martial art   a kind of fighting first used for combat or self-defense

What things are
special to your country?
What things are
the same as in Japan?

Explore Japan

Japan consists of four main islands and thousands of smaller islands. The islands are the tops of a mountain range that rises from the ocean floor. The land under the mountains moves a great deal. This movement causes earthquakes and volcanic eruptions. Thousands of earthquakes occur each year in Japan. Luckily, most of them are minor and don't cause much damage.

Japan has an imperial family. The Imperial Palace is in Tokyo and is home to Japan's emperor and his family. The ancient palace with its bridges, parks, and traditional architecture contrasts with the tall, modern buildings of Tokyo. The palace is open to visitors only two days a year. One of these days is the emperor's birthday.

imperial   relating to an empire, an emperor, or an empress

Tokyo is the capital of Japan. A famous city landmark is the Tokyo Tower. This structure is the tallest in Tokyo and resembles the Eiffel Tower in Paris.

On the Go!

Which mountain is the highest in Japan?
Go to page 16

What is the Japanese name for paper folding?
Go to page 21

What does the word *karate* mean?
Go to page 22

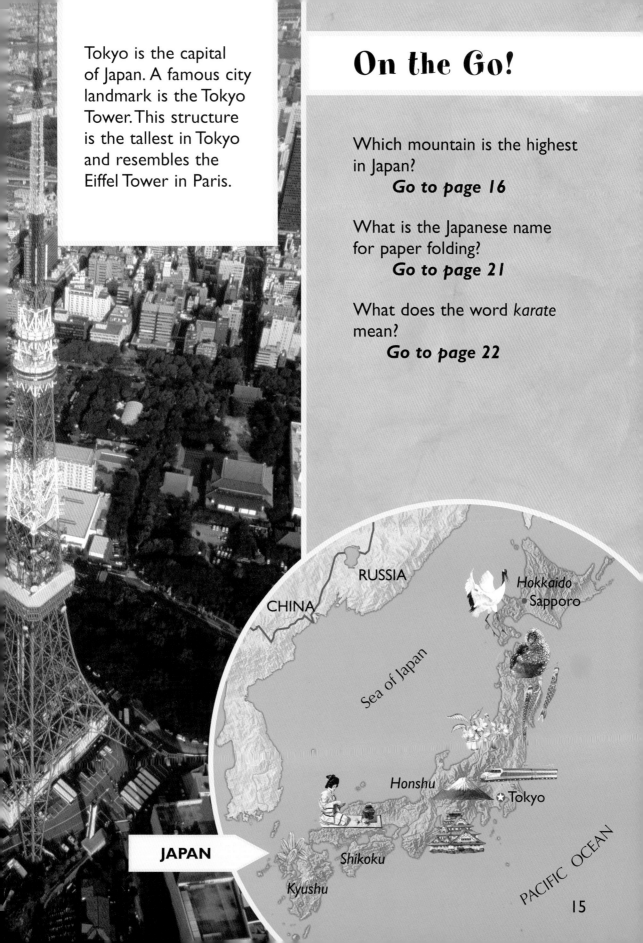

RUSSIA

CHINA

Hokkaido
Sapporo

Sea of Japan

Honshu

Tokyo

JAPAN

Shikoku

Kyushu

PACIFIC OCEAN

Tokyo

Tokyo is one of the largest and most crowded cities in the world. It is home to more than 12 million people. Like many other modern cities, Tokyo has tall buildings, museums, restaurants, sports stadiums, stores, and even a Disneyland theme park.

There are many things, however, that make Tokyo special. This modern city has ancient shrines, temples, and traditional Japanese gardens. There are also magnificent parks with cherry trees that blossom in spring. Perhaps the most amazing view of all, however, is the sight of Mount Fuji. This inactive volcano is located 60 miles away from Tokyo.

At nearly 12,390 feet, Mount Fuji is the highest mountain in Japan.

Limited land space in Tokyo has often caused housing shortages. Most people live in small apartments in tall buildings.

Tokyo by Train

Tokyo's busy subway stations have workers called pushers. It is their job to fill the trains with people. They push hundreds of commuters into each subway car.

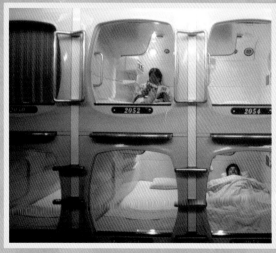

This hotel is called a capsule hotel. For people who travel to Tokyo on business, it is an inexpensive place to stay for the night.

High-Tech Japan

Japan is one of the leading manufacturing nations in the world. It has factories that use robots to help produce items such as automobiles. Today, Japan leads the way with clever designs in electronic and communication equipment, such as mobile phones.

High-tech toys are popular with the young people of Japan. They are also exported to other countries. Children of all ages enjoy electronic games, cartoon characters, and even robotic pets. These electronic pets are programmed to request things such as food and hugs from their young owners.

electronic devices powered by electricity

How do high tech toys
differ from other toys?

Japanese Arts

Many traditional arts are special to Japan. For instance, the art of flower arranging is known as ikebana (*ih keh BAH nah*). The aim of ikebana is to make an indoor arrangement look as if it were growing naturally outside. Gardening on a larger scale is also popular. Traditional Japanese gardens are works of art. They often have plants, ponds, rocks, and bridges. The gardens sometimes resemble a small scene from nature.

Other traditional art forms include growing bonsai (*BAHN sigh*), calligraphy, and origami.

Some people grow and shape tiny trees called bonsai. They remove new growth to stop the plant from growing to its usual size. Some bonsai are hundreds of years old.

Calligraphy, the ancient art of beautiful handwriting, is still taught in schools.

The ancient art of paper folding, or origami, is enjoyed by young and old.

Did You Know?

Long, slender wooden dolls have been made in Japan for hundreds of years. These traditional dolls have simple faces painted on them as well as flower designs. Some phone booths in Japan even have doll designs!

21

Martial Arts

Martial arts have been practiced for centuries in Japan, China, and other countries in Asia. In Japan, some of the techniques are based on the ancient fighting traditions of the samurai warriors.

Today, many people practice martial arts for health, fitness, and self-defense. Some martial arts, such as judo, don't use weapons. The unarmed competitors try to throw or pin down their opponents, relying on their skill and strength only. Karate students are also unarmed. In fact, the word *karate* means "empty hand."

Sumo wrestling is a traditional sport in Japan.
The massive wrestlers try to pin each other to
the ground or push one another outside the circle.

What do you do
to keep fit and healthy?
What is the history
behind that sport
or recreation?

Today, people around the
world practice judo (top)
and kendo.

23

What Do You Think?

1   Why do you think the people
of Japan still celebrate
the cherry blossom festival?

2   Cherry blossom festivals are held
in other parts of the world, too.
Why would this tradition
be celebrated outside of Japan?

**Why do you think
cherry blossom time
is an important time
for families and friends?**

Index